Fireworks, Picnics, and Flags

JAMES CROSS GIBLIN

illustrated by URSULA ARNDT

CLARION BOOKS

NEW YORK

Acknowledgment:
Special thanks to Independence National Historical
Park and the Free Library of Philadelphia

Clarion Books
a Houghton Mifflin Company imprint
215 Park Avenue South, New York, NY 10003
Text copyright © 1983 by James Cross Giblin
Illustrations copyright © 1983 by Ursula Arndt

Stanza from the song "Yankee Doodle Boy"
copyright by the George M. Cohan Music Publishing Co., Inc.
Used by permission.

www.houghtonmifflinbooks.com

Printed in the USA.

Library of Congress Cataloging-in-Publication Data

Giblin, James Cross.
Fireworks, picnics, and flags : the story of the Fourth of July symbols /
by James Cross Giblin ; illustrated by Ursula Arndt.
New York : Clarion Books [1983]
Summary: Traces the social history behind America's celebration of
Independence Day and explains the background of such national
symbols as the flag, the bald eagle, the Liberty Bell, and Uncle Sam.
ISBN 0-618-09652-3   PA ISBN 0-618-09654-X
1. Fourth of July celebrations—Juvenile literature. 2. American Revolution
Bicentennial, 1776–1976—Juvenile literature.
[1. Fourth of July] I. Arndt, Ursula, illus. II. Title
E286.A1297 1983   394.2'68473 19   82-009612

EB 10 9 8 7 6 5 4 3 2 1

Author's Note

I had the privilege of editing the six books Edna Barth wrote about the symbols of Easter, Christmas, Halloween, Thanksgiving, Valentine's Day, and St. Patrick's Day. Edna was intending to do a seventh on the Fourth of July symbols when she was struck by a fatal illness.

In deciding to research and write the book myself, I remembered something Edna told me when she was working on the first one, *Lilies, Rabbits, and Painted Eggs*: "I'm learning so much — and having such fun!" Now I know what she meant. I only hope young readers will have the same happy experience when they read this book.

J.C.G.

For my mother

Contents

Flags waving in the summer breeze. A man dressed as Uncle Sam leading a parade along Main Street. Patriotic music that makes your feet want to tap. Red, white, and blue fireworks exploding in the sky at night. All these things make us think of the Fourth of July, just as Santa Claus makes us think of Christmas and painted eggs make us think of Easter.

But the symbols of the Fourth of July are different. For the American flag and Uncle Sam and patriotic songs are not just part of our national birthday celebration. They are the symbols of our nation itself, and their story goes back to one of the most important events in our country's history: the adoption of the Declaration of Independence on July 4, 1776.

That is why the Fourth of July is often called Independence Day.

July 4, 1776

J uly 4, 1776, dawned clear and sunny in Philadelphia, where the Second Continental Congress was in session at the State House. Delegates from all of the thirteen American colonies were attending the Congress. That day they hoped to reach final agreement on America's Declaration of Independence from Great Britain.

Thomas Jefferson of Virginia, the man who had written the Declaration, stopped off on his way to the State House that morning to buy a new thermometer. In his diary, Jefferson noted that the highest temperature of the day was seventy-six degrees at one o'clock. But it probably seemed warmer in the Assembly Room of the State House because of the heated arguments taking place there.

The delegates to the Congress were going over the draft of the Declaration line by line, changing

2

a word here, crossing out a sentence there. Thomas Jefferson found it hard to sit quietly and listen while his manuscript was criticized.

The delegates from South Carolina and Georgia were especially upset by a paragraph in which Jefferson condemned the slave trade. After much discussion, it was deleted. Finally in late afternoon, the edited Declaration came to a vote. It was adopted 12 to 0, with New York abstaining. That colony wasn't yet ready to break all ties with Britain.

John Hancock, president of the Second Continental Congress, and Charles Thomson, its secretary, signed the Declaration that day. The rest of the delegates waited until August 2, when they signed a special copy written on parchment. It is the one that can be seen today at the National Archives in Washington, D.C.

After Hancock and Thomson had finished signing, the delegates ordered that copies of the Declaration be printed and sent to the governors of the colonies and the commanders of the American army. America had been involved in an undeclared war with Britain for over a year, although no major battles were being fought at the moment. As soon as they received their copies, the governors and army commanders would proclaim the Declaration to all the citizens and soldiers of the new United States.

There were no celebrations in Philadelphia on that first Fourth of July. No bells rang, no fireworks went off. They would come later. Instead, after Congress finished its work for the day, Thomas Jefferson went shopping and bought seven pairs of gloves as a present for his wife, Martha.

The Colonies Get Angry

☆ ☆ ☆

What led up to the Declaration of Independence? And why was this document so important that each year we celebrate the day it was adopted?

The conflict between the American colonies and their mother country, Great Britain, had been brewing for a long time. It started almost as soon as people from Britain began settling in North America in the 1600s.

The British government decreed that the colonies must sell their wood, furs, tobacco, and other products to Britain and Britain alone. The colonies protested, saying they should have the right to sell their products to whatever country offered the best prices for them.

The colonies also wanted to make their own clothing, furniture, and machinery. But the British Parliament insisted that they import all such

5

manufactured goods from Britain, almost 3,500 miles away.

What angered the colonies most, though, were the taxes that Parliament kept imposing on them. The American colonists saw no reason why they should pay taxes to Great Britain when they had no one to speak for them in Parliament. "No taxation without representation!" was the cry that went up whenever Britain tried to introduce a new tax.

The conflict first exploded into violence in Boston in 1770. Enraged by a British tax on paper, tea, and other imported goods, a crowd threw rocks and oyster shells at some British soldiers who were marching by. The soldiers turned and fired on the crowd, killing five people and wounding several others. News of the incident quickly spread throughout the colonies, and it came to be known as "the Boston Massacre."

In September 1774, delegates from twelve of the
thirteen colonies traveled to Philadelphia to attend
a meeting called the First Continental Congress.
Among other actions, the delegates urged that the
colonies refuse to buy British goods as a protest
against British policies.

Meanwhile, Britain was sending more and more
soldiers and weapons to the colonies. In case the
British soldiers made trouble, many American
towns and villages organized groups of minutemen. The minutemen were volunteers who

King George III.

promised to be ready for military duty at a minute's notice. However, most Americans were still loyal to Great Britain and its king, George III.

Then, in April 1775, the first armed clashes between British and American troops occurred at Lexington and Concord in Massachusetts.

General Thomas Gage, the royal governor of Massachusetts, sent British soldiers to seize military supplies the Americans had stored at Concord. Warned by Paul Revere, American minutemen resisted the British, first at Lexington and then at Concord. Shots were fired, and many soldiers and minutemen were killed or wounded. The American Revolution had begun.

A month later, in May 1775, the Second Continental Congress met in Philadelphia. It named George Washington commander-in-chief of the American armed forces. But it hesitated to make a final break with Britain, fearing that would mean all-out war. Instead the delegates sent a message to King George, telling him the colonies remained loyal. They listed all of their complaints against Parliament. And they begged the king to halt further British military moves, like the march on Lexington and Concord, while both sides tried to reach a peaceful settlement.

In those days news took six to eight weeks to travel each way across the Atlantic Ocean by ship. So it wasn't until September that Congress received the king's reply. He completely ignored the delegates' complaints and charged that the colonies were in a state of rebellion.

John Adams of Massachusetts and other New England leaders wanted to declare America's independence from Britain then and there. But many delegates from the Middle Atlantic and Southern colonies still hoped that the king and Parliament might change their attitude. Quite the contrary. In the spring of 1776, Parliament ordered British merchants to stop all trade with the colonies. It also authorized the British navy to seize any American ships they met at sea.

Parliament was trying to break the spirit of the

George
Washington

9

rebels. Instead its ban on trade only made more
Americans angry. Congress voted to arm American
vessels so that they could defend themselves if
British ships attacked them.

Many in Congress wanted to take even stronger
steps. On April 12, North Carolina instructed its
delegates to vote for independence from Great
Britain. Finally, on June 7, Richard Henry Lee of
Virginia rose in the State House in Philadelphia
and urged that Congress "declare the United Colonies free and independent states." John Adams
seconded the motion.

It soon became clear, however, that at least five
colonies were still not ready to vote in favor of independence. Congress knew the British would
never take Lee's resolution seriously if it were supported by only eight of the thirteen colonies. So
the members decided to postpone further discussion of the resolution until July 1.

Meanwhile, delegates from the five uncertain colonies agreed to ask the people in their districts how they felt about declaring America's independence from Great Britain. And a congressional committee was appointed to write a formal Declaration of Independence in case it was needed.

Five delegates served on the committee, including John Adams and Benjamin Franklin. But it was Thomas Jefferson who wrote the first draft of the Declaration by himself. The other committee members asked him to do so because Jefferson was known to be an excellent writer. As John Adams said later, "If George Washington was the sword of the Revolution, Thomas Jefferson was the pen."

Benjamin Franklin

Thomas Jefferson

John Adams

Richard Henry Lee

The Declaration of Independence

★ ★ ★

Thomas Jefferson was staying in two rented rooms in the house of Jacob Graff, a brick-layer, a few blocks from the State House. The Graff house has been restored, and visitors today can see a portable writing table like the one on which Jefferson wrote the Declaration of Independence with quill pens. Although Jefferson drew on the ideas of many other thinkers and writers, he wrote the Declaration without referring to any books or pamphlets. It took him two and a half weeks to complete.

Debate on Richard Henry Lee's resolution started again in Congress on July 1. A first vote showed nine of the thirteen colonies now in favor of independence. Pennsylvania and South Carolina both voted "No." The delegates from Delaware and New York disagreed among themselves, so those two colonies abstained.

South Carolina's delegates said their colony would vote for independence if Pennsylvania and Delaware could be persuaded to change their votes. John Adams, Richard Henry Lee, and other supporters of independence quickly went to work. They talked to the four out of seven Pennsylvania delegates who were opposed to the Declaration, trying to get them to change their minds.

They also sent a fast rider on the eighty-mile trip to the farm of Caesar Rodney, Delaware's third delegate. Rodney, a strong supporter of independence, had stayed away from the session because he was suffering from cancer. But he listened carefully as the rider explained the situation and told Rodney how much his vote was needed.

Tuesday, July 2, was gray and humid in Philadelphia. Flies and mosquitoes annoyed the delegates in the State House while they continued to debate Lee's resolution. Two of the Pennsylvania delegates who were opposed to independence stayed home that day. As a result, Pennsylvania's vote would be 3 to 2 in favor.

Shortly after lunch, Caesar Rodney hurried into the Assembly Room. He had been riding since

daybreak in order to reach the State House in time. Even though he was exhausted, Rodney asked to speak as soon as possible. He said, "As I believe the voice of all sensible and honest men is in favor of Independence, and my own judgment concurs with them, I vote for Independence!"

Thus Delaware voted "Yes" along with Pennsylvania. South Carolina swung in line behind the two, as its delegates had promised to do the day before. And Lee's resolution passed 12 to 0, with only New York abstaining. That afternoon the United Colonies became the United States of America.

Overjoyed, John Adams wrote to his wife: "I believe that the second day of July, 1776, will be celebrated by succeeding generations as the great anniversary festival. . . . It ought to be solemnized with pomp and parade, with shows, games, sports, guns, bells, bonfires, and illuminations, from one end of this continent to the other, from this time forward, forevermore."

Congress wasn't as ready to celebrate as Adams. It had voted for independence, but it hadn't yet approved the document that would explain its decision to the world. All during July 3 and most of

July 4 the delegates discussed the wording of Thomas Jefferson's Declaration of Independence.

The final text was adopted on the fourth, as we have seen. But the citizens of Philadelphia didn't celebrate the event until four days later, on July 8. That morning the Declaration was published in the city's newspapers. And at noon it was read aloud for the first time in the yard behind the State House.

Colonel John Nixon, commander of the city guard, had been chosen as the speaker because of his powerful voice. Nixon stood on a high wooden platform and began to read: "We hold these truths to be self-evident, that all men are created equal, that they are endowed by their Creator with certain inalienable rights, that among these are Life, Liberty, and the Pursuit of Happiness."

The Declaration went on to list all of the unfair and unjust things King George and the British Parliament had done to the colonies. It told how the colonies had pleaded unsuccessfully with the king to change his policies. And it ended by stating "That these United Colonies are, and of Right ought to be, FREE AND INDEPENDENT STATES; that they are absolved from all Allegiance to the British Crown, and that all political Connection between them and the State of Great Britain, is and ought to be totally dissolved."

A large crowd in the State House yard listened to the stirring words of the Declaration. Delaware Indians in colorful robes stood next to Quakers wearing broad-brimmed black hats. Recent immigrants from England, Ireland, and Germany mingled with sailors whose ships were tied up at the city's docks. There weren't many well-to-do citizens in the crowd, though. Most of them had business ties with Britain, and still supported the mother country.

After Colonel Nixon had finished, the audience cheered loudly. "God Bless the Free States of America!" someone shouted. Nine men rushed inside the State House and ripped down the king's coat-of-arms from the wall of the Supreme Court Chamber. That night the coat of arms was carried to a nearby park. There it was placed atop a bonfire and burned while a crowd applauded.

According to John Adams, the bells of Philadelphia rang all day on July 8 and most of the night, too. The bell on top of the State House — the one that came to be known as the Liberty Bell — chimed with the others.

Similar celebrations took place throughout the colonies when riders delivered the printed copies of the Declaration. Cannons roared, soldiers paraded, bonfires blazed. And in many places something connected with British rule was burned or destroyed.

In New York City, General George Washington ordered the Declaration to be read aloud to his troops on July 9. Afterward a mob, including some soldiers, toppled a statue of King George riding a horse and smashed it into little pieces. They said they did it so that the lead in the statue could be melted down and made into bullets for Washington's army. But Washington himself was not pleased. He thought the act showed a lack of self-discipline.

In Savannah, Georgia, which was deep in the South and one of the last places to receive a copy of the Declaration, the citizens celebrated all day long. Then they staged a mock funeral procession and buried a likeness of King George in front of the Court House.

Although they didn't know it, the delegates to the Second Continental Congress had declared independence just in time. For the British general William Howe had landed 10,000 troops on Staten Island on July 2 and was getting ready to attack George Washington's forces in New York. The Revolutionary War was about to begin in earnest.

We could celebate our national birthday, our Independence Day, on any one of several different dates. It could be July 2, when the Second Continental Congress voted in favor of independence. Or July 4, when the Congress adopted the Declaration of Independence. Or July 8, when the Declaration was first read aloud. Why was July 4 chosen?

Probably to focus people's attention on the *meaning* of the Declaration. For that document did more than just declare our independence from Great Britain. It also stated that the government of a country should rule according to the wishes of its citizens, and with their consent. If a government failed to do so, as the British had failed in America, then the citizens had a right to revolt against it and "provide new guards for their future security."

By establishing these principles, the Declaration laid the foundation for a free, democratic government in the United States. It also served as an inspiration for people in many other countries who longed to be free. As President Abraham Lincoln said in 1861, "The Declaration of Independence gave liberty not alone to the people of this country, but hope to all of the world for all future time."

FREEDOM TO SPEAK OUT

20

The Holiday Takes Shape

☆ ☆ ☆

A year later, in 1777, bells rang all day in Philadelphia on July 4. The city where the Declaration of Independence was first read aloud was also the city where the first Fourth of July celebrations were held.

The citizens had reason to celebrate. Even though the British army occupied New York City and was threatening Philadelphia from the south, the Revolutionary War was not going badly. General George Washington had struck back successfully the winter before in battles at Trenton and Princeton, New Jersey. And Britain's old enemy, France, had agreed to help the struggling American army with men and supplies. Those who feared the Americans would quickly collapse in the face of superior British forces had been proved wrong.

At noon on July 4, warships along the Philadelphia docks fired a thirteen-gun salute in honor of the thirteen United States. That afternoon many members of Congress, which had been dismissed for the day, attended a grand dinner at City Tavern. A Philadelphia newspaper editor proposed the main toast: "Thus may the Fourth of July, that glorious and memorable day, be celebrated through America by the sons of freedom from age to age, till time shall be no more."

After the dinner, all soldiers who were stationed in Philadelphia paraded through the streets. Large crowds cheered them. That evening bonfires were lit and fireworks exploded in the night sky.

Many families put lighted candles in their windows to celebrate the Fourth and to show their support for the ongoing Revolutionary War. "It was the most splendid illumination I ever saw," John Adams wrote to his wife in Massachusetts.

However, all was not bright and peaceful in Philadelphia that night. People loyal to Great Brit-

ain deliberately left their windows dark, and angry patriots hurled rocks through many of them.

Other places in the new United States soon began to celebrate the Fourth of July.

The first celebrations in Boston took place on July 4, 1783, the year the Revolutionary War ended. Up until then, Boston's main patriotic holiday had been the anniversary of the Boston Massacre on March 5.

Boston started what became a Fourth of July tradition by having a well-known speaker deliver a patriotic oration on the holiday. In 1783 the speaker was Dr. John Warren. His brother, General Joseph Warren, had been killed at the Battle of Bunker Hill early in the Revolution. Like other Fourth of July orators, Warren recalled the heroism of George Washington and his soldiers. He hailed the growth of the United States and described the great future that lay before the country now that the war was over.

Philadelphia staged a huge celebration on July 4, 1788. It honored not only the holiday but also the U.S. Constitution, which had just been ratified by ten states.

At 9:00 A.M. a grand parade, more than a mile and a half in length, began to march through the streets of Philadelphia. The city was then the capital of the United States. It was the home of the Supreme Court as well as Congress.

The justices of the Supreme Court rode on a horse-drawn float shaped like a giant eagle. Other floats dramatized the Fourth of July 1776 and the new Constitution. The parade lasted for more than three hours. Afterward a picnic lunch was served to the marchers.

Fourth of July speakers often talked about the need for unity in the United States. But in many places the day was marred by outbursts of violence. The Federalists, who supported the Constitution and the idea of a strong central government, clashed with the Republicans, who thought the individual states should have the most power. There were many arguments and fights. In Boston in 1806, a supporter of states' rights was murdered by a Federalist leader on the Fourth of July.

For most Americans, though, the Fourth was a happy day, filled with feasting and fun. A poem published in a New Hampshire newspaper gives a

good picture of how the holiday was celebrated in the early 1800s:

> Squeak the fife and beat the drum,
> Independence Day is come!
> Quickly rub the pewter platter,
> Heap the nut cakes fried in batter,
> Set the cups and beaker glass,
> The pumpkin and the apple sauce . . .
> . . . Thus we dance and thus we play,
> On glorious Independence Day!

During the War of 1812, when the United States fought Britain for the second time, Fourth of July speeches were especially patriotic. After the war ended in 1814, the Fourth became a day when important events were scheduled. Governor DeWitt Clinton of New York started this tradition by digging the first shovelful of earth for the Erie Canal on July 4, 1817.

The year 1826 marked the 50th anniversary of the Declaration of Independence. By then America stretched from Massachusetts in the East to the Oregon Territory on the West Coast. There were now twenty-four states in the Union, two of them beyond the Mississippi River. The population of the country stood at twelve million — four times what it had been on the first Fourth of July.

People wanted to observe the 50th anniversary in a dignified manner. As one newspaper editor put it, "Let's not celebrate in the usual way, that is, by frying chickens, firing away damaged powder, or fiddling our noses over tavern wine." All across the country plans were made for picnics, parades, and public readings of the Declaration of Independence.

Washington, D.C., had replaced Philadelphia as the nation's capital in 1800. So the mayor of Washington invited all the living signers of the Declaration, and all living ex-Presidents, to attend a special ceremony there on July 4. Unfortunately, none of the men was able to come, but they all wrote letters to the mayor.

Thomas Jefferson's was the most eloquent. At the end of the letter, he referred to the Declaration and the human rights that it guaranteed. "Let the annual return of this day refresh our recollections of these rights," the eighty-three-year-old Jefferson wrote, "and our undiminished devotion to them."

The White House in 1826

President John Quincy Adams, son of John Adams, marveled at the force of Jefferson's letter. Within a few days it was printed in the Washington newspapers, and later it was reprinted all over the United States.

Meanwhile, John Adams had also been invited to attend the Fourth of July celebrations in Quincy, Massachusetts, where he was living in retirement. Adams was then ninety, and too frail to go. However, he wrote a toast for the occasion: "Independence Forever!"

Late in the morning of July 4, a military parade saluted the President at the White House in Washington. Then the President joined the march to the Capitol where the Marine Band played and the Declaration of Independence was read.

Two days later, word reached Washington that Thomas Jefferson had died quietly in his Virginia home at noon on the Fourth. That was when the ceremonies at the Capitol were at their height. President Adams noted in his diary that Jefferson's dying on the Fourth was "a strange and very striking coincidence."

Then, on July 8, President Adams received several letters from Massachusetts, the latest written on the morning of the Fourth. The letters said that his father, John, was gravely ill.

Early on the morning of the ninth, the President set out for Massachusetts by carriage. But on the way he got word that his father was already dead. John Adams had passed away about five o'clock in the afternoon on the Fourth, just a few hours after Thomas Jefferson.

People had been stunned when they learned that Jefferson had died on July 4. They were even more shocked when they heard that Adams had died on that day, too. Some thought the two deaths revealed the will of God at work.

In the days and weeks that followed, many tributes to the two men appeared in the newspapers. Everyone remembered the democratic ideals for which they both had fought in July 1776. As long as those ideals endured, so would the spirit of Jefferson and Adams.

By 1826 the basic pattern of the Fourth of July was taking shape. Already it was a day of picnics and parades, of fireworks and patriotic speeches. Soon all the symbols of the new nation — the flag, patriotic music and art, Uncle Sam, the Liberty Bell — would begin to play their part in Fourth of July celebrations, too.

The Flag

★ ★ ★

From dawn to dusk on the Fourth of July, the American flag flies from homes and public buildings.

Today the flag has seven red stripes and six white ones, and fifty white stars on a blue square. The thirteen stripes stand for the thirteen original colonies, and the stars represent the fifty states. The design and colors of the flag have inspired many nicknames. Some people call it the Stars and Stripes, others the Star-Spangled Banner, and others simply the Red, White, and Blue.

Because the flag is so familiar, we may think it has always been the same. But before the Revolution, there was no single American flag. Each colony, and many military regiments, had their own flags or banners, just as each state has its own flag today. These colonial flags featured many different

29

DON'T TREAD ON ME

AN APPEAL TO HEAVEN

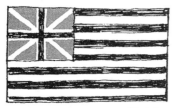

GRAND UNION FLAG

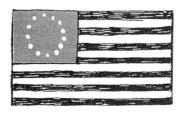

FLAG, adopted
June 14, 1777

emblems. On one was a rifleman, on another a beaver, and on another a coiled rattlesnake. They carried slogans such as "Liberty or Death," "Conquer or Die," and "Don't Tread on Me!"

Our first national flag was raised on a hill near Boston on January 4, 1776, by troops serving under General George Washington. It was called the Grand Union flag and had thirteen red and blue stripes. But instead of stars it displayed the crosses of Saint Andrew and Saint George, the symbols of Great Britain. For in January 1776, America was still officially tied to Britain.

After the Declaration of Independence, the American people wanted to have a purely American flag. The Second Continental Congress adopted a design for one on June 14, 1777, the day we now celebrate as Flag Day. The congressional resolution stated "That the flag of the United States be 13 stripes, alternately red and white, and that the Union be 13 stars, white in a blue field, representing a new constellation."

For a long time, people believed that Betsy Ross, an upholsterer and flagmaker in Philadelphia, made the first of the new American flags. Her grandson claimed that George Washington himself had given her the assignment. But Washington was off fighting the British in New Jersey at the time he was supposed to have called on Betsy

Ross. What is probably true is that she was one of several Philadelphia flagmakers who made examples of the new flag in 1777.

Congress also passed a resolution that each time a new state was added to the Union, a new star and a new stripe would be added to the flag. After Vermont joined the Union in 1791 and Kentucky in 1792, the flag had fifteen stars and fifteen stripes. This was the flag that Francis Scott Key saw flying over Fort McHenry, Maryland, during the War of 1812 — the flag that inspired him to write "The Star-Spangled Banner."

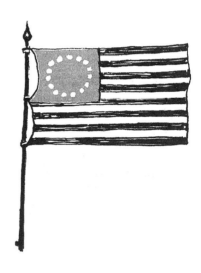

After the War of 1812 ended in 1814, many new states wanted to join the Union. Congress realized that if both a new star and a new stripe were added for each state, the flag would become too large. So in 1818 it decided that the flag would always have just thirteen stripes, but that a star would still be added for each new state. The addition of the star would take place on the Fourth of July following the state's admission into the Union.

By 1912, when Arizona and New Mexico entered the Union, the flag had forty-eight stars. The number remained the same until 1959, when Alaska became a state. That Fourth of July, just after midnight, a flag with forty-nine stars was raised for the first time over Fort McHenry in Maryland.

A year later, on July 4, 1960, a new flag with fifty stars was hoisted over Fort McHenry at 12:01 A.M. This flag marked Hawaii's entry into the Union, and it is the one we salute today.

The flag has always had a special meaning for Americans in wartime. When the Civil War began in 1861, the South adopted its own flag. But the North did not remove the stars of the Southern states from the U.S. flag. People in the North had faith that someday all the states would be together again.

On July 4, 1862, many Northern soldiers were being held as prisoners of war at Libby Prison in Richmond, Virginia. The soldiers wanted to celebrate the Fourth, but they had no flag. So they secretly made one from a pair of blue flannel trousers and a piece of red cloth. They used a white shirt for the stars and the stripes. Early on the morning of the Fourth the soldiers managed to raise the homemade flag above their barracks. It waved for almost an hour before the prison guards saw it and made the soldiers take it down.

During World War I and World War II, Americans felt unusually patriotic. Almost everyone believed we were fighting on the side of right, and the Stars and Stripes were proudly displayed on the Fourth of July.

The nation's mood was different during the Vietnam War of the late 1960s and early 1970s. Many people disagreed with our government's policies. Some stopped flying the flag on the Fourth and other holidays as a show of protest.

The country experienced a new sense of pride in July 1969, when our astronauts landed on the moon and erected a U.S. flag at their base site. This flag was made of metal, not cloth. It needed to be sturdy so that it would withstand the dust and rock particles from space that constantly bombard the moon's surface.

The nation's spirits rose even higher on July 4, 1976, when we celebrated the 200th anniversary of the Declaration of Independence. Flagmakers reported that there had never been such a great demand for flags as there was that year.

In July 1981, the largest American flag ever made was displayed on a softball field in New York City's Central Park. The flag measured 411 feet by 211 feet, and each of its fifty stars was 13 feet wide. It covered two acres and weighed seven tons.

Textile companies, dye manufacturers, and engineering firms all helped to make this giant flag, which is a project of the Great American Flag Fund. The Fund hopes the flag will capture peoples' imaginations and remind them of America's accomplishments. As soon as the Fund raises the money for special rigging, the huge flag will fly from the Verrazano-Narrows Bridge at the entrance to New York Harbor. It will be unfurled on all of our national holidays, and will be visible for miles.

From 1777 until now, most Americans have felt a special thrill when they saw our flag waving in the breeze on the Fourth of July. President Woodrow Wilson suggested why people feel this way in a speech he made during World War I. Wilson said: "This flag, which we honor, and under which we serve, is the emblem of our unity, our power, our thought, and our purpose as a nation."

Fireworks

★ ★ ★

Starting early in the morning on the Fourth of July, firecrackers can be heard popping and snapping in the streets of many American towns and cities. In the evening, crowds gather to watch fireworks explode in colorful patterns against the night sky.

No one knows who invented fireworks. Some say they were first used by the Chinese, and were brought back to Europe by the Italian explorer Marco Polo. Others say the Arabs were the first to explode them. Yet another story claims that a German magician invented them in the 1300s. What is known is that people have celebrated with fireworks for over six hundred years.

All fireworks, large and small, go off with a bang because they contain a substance called black powder. It is similar to gunpowder. In a firecracker, the black powder is packed into a small roll of paper

35

and a fuse is attached. When the fuse is lit and the flame reaches the powder, the firecracker explodes.

The fireworks used in aerial displays are more complicated. First black powder is mixed with metallic salts that produce colors when they burn. This mixture is then compressed into small pellets called "stars," and the stars are packed into a tube called a "shell." The shell is made of papier-mâché, clay, or some other substance that burns easily.

When it's time for the fireworks display, the shell is placed in a short cannon called a mortar and rocketed high in the air with a lift charge. A special time fuse then ignites the stars within the shell one by one. A large shell may contain hundreds of stars, each of which leaves behind a different trail of color when it explodes. If the mixture in the star includes calcium salts, the trail will be red. Aluminum or magnesium salts produce a white trail, and copper salts a blue one.

Because they are filled with explosives, fireworks have always been dangerous to handle. In the Middle Ages, experienced fireworks handlers, called "firemasters," were much in demand at the royal courts of Europe. Firemasters designed the elaborate fireworks that were shot off to celebrate military victories, religious festivals, and the crowning of kings or queens.

By the 1700s, most firemasters had helpers who

were known as "wild men" or "green men." They wore caps of green leaves on their heads. Like jesters, the green men ran through crowds, telling stories and making jokes. They warned people to stand back, and then set off fireworks with lighted sticks called fire clubs. Many green men were injured or killed when their fireworks went off too soon or failed to rise into the air.

Fireworks experts from Italy, France, and other European countries brought their knowledge to America in the mid-1800s. Soon fireworks became an important part of Fourth of July celebrations all across the country. And people everywhere began to complain about the noise fireworks made and the damage they caused.

On July 4, 1866, a resident of Germantown, Pennsylvania, wrote in his diary: "July 4th is the most hateful day of the year, when the birth of democracy is celebrated by license and noise. All last night and all of today, the sound of guns and firecrackers around us never stopped. It is difficult to feel patriotic on the Fourth of July."

In the 1890s, the "Society for the Suppression of Unnecessary Noise" was founded. It tried to get laws passed outlawing the use of firecrackers near hospitals and other public buildings on the Fourth of July. But still the violence continued. People put firecrackers under milk bottles, flowerpots, or tin cans and sent them shooting up into the air. Sometimes they threw lighted firecrackers at passing horses and laughed when the animals reared up in fright.

To prove their courage, children and grownups, too, would often light a firecracker, hold it between thumb and forefinger, and wait to throw it until the fuse was almost gone. Sometimes they waited too long, and the firecracker would go off in their hands, burning or maiming them.

The American Medical Association kept records of the deaths and injuries caused by holiday fireworks between 1903 and 1907. On the Fourth during those years, 1,153 people were killed and 21,520 others were injured. When these statistics were published, opponents of fireworks said that the lyrics of a well-known patriotic song should be changed as follows: "My country 'tis of thee, / For thou hast crippled me!"

In 1903 the city of Springfield, Massachusetts, outlawed the sale of fireworks. As a result, there were no injuries or fires in Springfield on the Fourth of July that year. Other cities and states followed Springfield's example, and fireworks soon became illegal in many sections of the country.

Fireworks today are legal for general use in only thirty-five of the fifty states. Even where they are legal, there are often restrictions on their sale. In

California, for example, they can be sold only during the week before the Fourth of July. And they must be "safe and sane fireworks" that cannot explode and do not rise into the air when they are lit.

Large firecrackers such as cherry bombs have been banned nationwide since 1966. The ban is enforced by the Treasury Department's Bureau of Alcohol, Tobacco, and Firearms. Each year the Bureau raids at least half a dozen factories making illegal fireworks. After a raid, Bureau agents defuse the fireworks they have found by dousing them with water and detergent and burying them.

Two-thirds of the fireworks used in the United States today are imported from China, Japan, South Korea, Taiwan, and other countries. The U.S. Customs Service checks to make sure that all of them are safe.

Imported fireworks are famous for their beautiful colors and are often used in nighttime fireworks displays on the Fourth of July. These displays are legal everywhere, even in states such as New York that outlaw the sale of fireworks to the general public.

The displays are staged by experts like the firemasters of the Middle Ages. But today's fireworks are music- and color-coordinated, and electronically timed. Each year they soar higher into the sky and last longer.

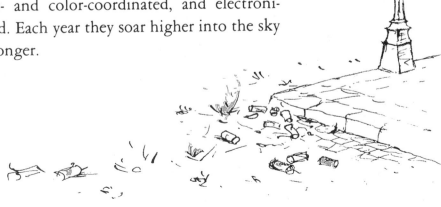

As red, white, and blue sparks shower down, crowds from Washington, D.C., to San Francisco are reminded of the Declaration of Independence and the events of the first July 4. John Adams's prediction that our national birthday would be celebrated with "illuminations" has come true.

"The Spirit of '76"

O n the Fourth of July, patriotic paintings and drawings are often published on the front pages of newspapers. The painting that probably appears more frequently than any other is called *The Spirit of '76.*

There are three figures in the painting, all of them playing musical instruments. A white-haired old man beats a drum, a middle-aged man with a bandaged head plays a fife, and a young drummer boy looks admiringly at the old drummer. Behind them marches a company of Revolutionary soldiers. One of the soldiers is carrying the first American flag.

Archibald Willard, the man who painted *The Spirit of '76,* lived in the small town of Wellington, Ohio, and worked in a carriage factory. In his spare time he painted landscapes and humorous pictures. On July 4, 1871, he got the idea for the

painting that was to bring him worldwide fame.

Early that morning, Willard saw three boys — two drummers and a fife player — getting ready to march in the Wellington holiday parade. One drummer was juggling his sticks, and all three were good-humoredly bumping into one another. Willard made a quick pencil sketch of the boys, and meant to do a painting of them later.

A friend who saw the sketch gave Willard a different idea. Instead of a comic scene, the friend suggested that Willard paint a serious picture with a patriotic theme. The artist was intrigued. It would be unlike anything he had ever done.

As he planned the painting, Willard remembered stories told him by his grandfather, who had fought in the Revolutionary War. They helped him decide what figures to include. Willard's own father posed as the old drummer, and a Civil War comrade of Willard's posed as the fife player. Henry Devereaux, the thirteen-year-old son of a railroad president, was the model for the drummer boy.

The large painting, eight by ten feet, was com-

pleted early in 1876. That year marked the centennial of the Declaration of Independence. Willard heard there would be an exhibit of paintings at the grand Centennial Exhibition in Philadelphia. He decided to submit *The Spirit of '76*.

The Centennial Commission had said that only classical paintings from the major art centers of Europe and America would be eligible for the exhibit. But when the Commission members saw Willard's painting, they were so moved that they accepted it at once. *The Spirit of '76* quickly became one of the most popular pictures in the entire exhibit. It attracted such large crowds that special guards were assigned to protect it.

After the Centennial Exhibition closed, General Devereaux, the father of the model for the drummer boy, bought the painting from Archibald Willard. Then he sent it on a long tour of the country. It finally came to rest in Marblehead, Massachusetts, General Devereaux's birthplace. There it can be seen today.

Over the past one hundred years, *The Spirit of '76* has been reproduced on china plates, towels, and napkins, as well as on posters and greeting cards. It has come to symbolize the courage of Revolutionary War soldiers, who were willing to fight for America's right to govern itself. And it reminds people everywhere of why we celebrate Independence Day.

43

Fourth of July Picnics

⭐ ⭐ ⭐

Feasting has always been part of Fourth of July celebrations. On July 4, 1777, grand banquets were held in Philadelphia and other cities. But soon the parties moved outdoors.

The weather all over America is usually warm on the Fourth. If it doesn't rain, it's a perfect day for a picnic. By the middle of the 19th century, the Fourth of July picnic had become a national tradition.

In the morning, a family would gather in their kitchen to pack the picnic baskets. Into them went crispy pieces of fried chicken, bowls of potato salad, containers of lemonade, chocolate and angel food cakes, and pickles of all sorts — sweet, dill, and watermelon-rind.

There were also plenty of the family's favorite, deviled eggs. These were shelled hard-boiled eggs, cut lengthwise, from which the yellow yolks had

44

been removed. The yolks were crumbled and mixed with mayonnaise, mustard, bits of celery or onions, and salt and pepper. Then this mixture was put back in the whites of the eggs. Delicious!

Another favorite dish was homemade ice cream. It was made with real farm cream in a hand-turned freezer, surrounded by chopped ice and rock salt. Everyone in the family helped to turn the freezer. The one who made the most turns got to lick the inside of the barrel that contained the ice cream.

After all the food was ready, the baskets were loaded into the family buggy, and everyone climbed in. Father called "Gee-up!" to the horse, and the family was off to the picnic grove.

Almost every town, large and small, had a picnic grove. It was usually located in a pleasant, shady spot beside a river or lake. Nearby there was always a field, like the parking lots of today, where people could leave their horses and buggies.

Fourth of July picnics were organized in different ways. Sometimes a single family would set out and have a picnic on its own. Other times a group such as a Sunday school would sponsor the picnic. Forty or fifty families would attend, each bringing different dishes. Then everyone would sample as many dishes as possible.

In the late 1800s, political campaigns began on the Fourth of July, and local politicians often sponsored holiday picnics. The picnickers sat on folding chairs or blankets and listened to long political speeches. In return they got free frankfurters, corn on the cob, and sometimes steamed clams. There was pink lemonade for the women and children, and draft beer for the men.

After the eating was over, the games began. The men might engage in a tug-of-war over a two-foot-deep mudhole. The children might chase after a greased pig. Everyone, young and old, competed in sack races and watermelon-eating contests.

By late afternoon, most people were ready to go home. They piled the empty picnic baskets into their buggies and took their seats. Everyone was a little tired and a little sunburned, but happy and full of good food. It had been a fine Fourth of July picnic.

Today few Sunday schools sponsor picnics on July 4, and most political campaigns don't get under way until Labor Day. But many families pack picnic baskets, climb into their cars, and head for a state park or a beach.

After they finish eating, people today are more likely to play a game of softball than enter a tug-of-war. But in some places there are still sack races and watermelon-eating contests.

Despite present-day traffic jams and crowded parks, most people would agree with their great-great-grandparents that Fourth of July picnics are lots of fun!

Patriotic Music and Songs

⭐ ⭐ ⭐

In many communities, people march in Fourth of July parades. Often there are holiday concerts by high school bands or professional orchestras. At all of these events, patriotic music is performed and patriotic songs are sung.

Among the most frequently played pieces in Fourth of July parades and concerts are the marches of John Philip Sousa. Born in 1854, Sousa was the son of a trombonist in the U.S. Marine Band. As a boy, he often heard his father play in military parades, and he developed a love for march music. When he was thirteen, he enlisted in the Marine Band as an apprentice.

Sousa quickly proved his worth and was appointed Director of the Band when he was only twenty-six. Soon thereafter he wrote the stirring Marine Corps hymn "Semper Fidelis" (Always Faithful). Later Sousa formed his own band,

48

which toured the United States, Canada, and Europe, giving more than ten thousand concerts. Besides conducting the band, Sousa composed over a hundred marches and became known as "the March King."

Some of John Philip Sousa's most popular marches are "Hands Across the Sea," "The Washington Post March," and "Stars and Stripes Forever." The last is often played as the final number in Fourth of July band concerts.

49

☆

Another composer whose works are closely linked with the Fourth of July is George M. Cohan. That's not surprising since Cohan, the son of two traveling entertainers, was born on July 4, 1878.

"From my earliest days I was impressed with the fact that I had been born under the Stars and Stripes," Cohan once said. "And that has a great deal to do with everything I have written."

One of Cohan's most famous songs — and one that is often played on the Fourth — is "Yankee Doodle Boy." Its lyrics begin:

I'm a Yankee Doodle Dandy,
A Yankee Doodle do or die;
A real live nephew of my Uncle Sam's,
Born on the Fourth of July.

Cohan wrote the stories, music, and lyrics for twenty Broadway musicals. He was also the producer, the director, and often the star of these shows. Among his popular songs are "Give My Regards to Broadway," "You're a Grand Old Flag," and "Over There," which became a famous battle song during World War I.

In 1936 Cohan was awarded a Congressional Medal of Honor for his patriotic songs. And in 1942 a movie musical was made about his life, *Yankee Doodle Dandy,* starring James Cagney. It is often shown on television on July 4, and still

moves people with its lively, toe-tapping songs.

At Fourth of July concerts, there usually comes a point when the audience is invited to sing along. Then the most familiar patriotic songs are played — songs like "Yankee Doodle," "America," and "The Star-Spangled Banner." Almost everyone knows the lyrics to these songs. But not everyone knows how they happened to be written, or what the lyrics originally meant.

The oldest of our patriotic songs is "Yankee Doodle." The word *Yankee* probably came from the first Dutch settlers in America. *Janke* — pronounced "Yankee" — is the familiar form of the Dutch name Jan, just as Johnny is the familiar form of John. The word *doodle* meant a foolish fellow, a simpleton.

The lyrics for "Yankee Doodle" were written in 1758 by Dr. Richard Shuckburg, a British army doctor who was serving in the American colonies. Like many of the British, Shuckburg looked down on the poorly dressed, poorly educated Americans who came to enlist in the British army. He made fun of these volunteers in the lyrics for "Yankee Doodle."

Yankee Doodle came to town
Riding on a pony,
He stuck a feather in his cap
And called it macaroni.

Shuckburg's joke backfired, though. Americans liked the song and added lyrics of their own. Twenty years later, during the Revolutionary War, they whistled the tune of "Yankee Doodle" as they marched into battle.

Here is a stanza that was added to the song during the Revolution:

"Yankee Doodle" is the tune
Americans delight in;
It suits for feasts, it suits for fun,
And just as well for fighting.

52

"Yankee Doodle" was sung during the first Independence Day celebrations in Philadelphia on July 4, 1777. And it is still sung proudly on the Fourth of July today.

☆

My country, 'tis of thee,
Sweet land of liberty,
Of thee I sing:
Land where my fathers died,
Land of the Pilgrims' pride,
From every mountainside
Let freedom ring.

Those familiar words were written in 1832 by Samuel Francis Smith, a student in Andover, Massachusetts, who later became a Baptist minister and editor.

A friend had given Smith a book of German songs to translate. Smith liked one tune so much that he was inspired to write a patriotic lyric of his own to go with it. Within half an hour he jotted down on a scrap of paper the verses of "America" that we still sing today.

"America" was first sung in public on July 4, 1831, in a special service at Boston's Park Street Congregational Church. Some people in the audience that day recognized a curious fact. The tune

of "America" was the same as the tune for the British hymn "God Save the King (or Queen)."

Smith was embarrassed. He hadn't known about the British song when he wrote the words for "America."

Despite that strange coincidence, "America" quickly became popular throughout the United States. It remains popular today, especially on the Fourth of July.

On a summer day in 1893, Katharine Lee Bates, an English professor at Wellesley College, journeyed to the top of Pike's Peak in Colorado. Standing there, 14,000 feet above sea level, she was overwhelmed by the view. To the west and north rose the towering Rockies. To the east, the Great Plains seemed to stretch forever.

Back in her hotel room that evening, Ms. Bates remembered everything she had seen. She took out her notebook and wrote the first draft of a poem. It began with these words:

> *O beautiful for spacious skies,*
> *For amber waves of grain,*
> *For purple mountain majesties*
> *Above the fruited plain!*

Ms. Bates titled her poem "America the Beautiful" and sent it to *The Congregationalist,* a religious

magazine. It was published in the issue of July 4, 1895, and won much praise. People urged that it be made into a song, and Ms. Bates chose the music of the hymn "Materna."

Today "America the Beautiful" is one of our favorite anthems. It is frequently sung on radio and television, and is almost always featured in Fourth of July celebrations.

One song, and one song alone, is never left out of any Independence Day program. That song is our national anthem, "The Star-Spangled Banner."

The verses of "The Star-Spangled Banner" tell a true story that happened near Baltimore, Maryland, on September 13 and 14, 1814. At that time America and Britain were still fighting the War of 1812. The British had seized a well-known American physician, Dr. William Beanes. They were holding him captive aboard their flagship in Chesapeake Bay.

Francis Scott Key

Beanes's friends hired Francis Scott Key, a young Washington lawyer, to try to secure the doctor's release. Key galloped to Baltimore, where he rented a small boat. Then he sailed down Chesapeake Bay, past Fort McHenry, to the place where the British flagship was anchored.

After talking with Key, the British admiral agreed to free Dr. Beanes. But he told Key that he and the doctor could not leave until later. The British fleet planned to launch an attack on Baltimore at dawn, and the admiral was afraid Key and Dr. Beanes would inform the Americans if he let them go beforehand.

The British fired the first shot on Fort McHenry at 6:00 A.M. on September 13, and the attack continued for twenty-five hours without letup. Francis Scott Key and Dr. Beanes watched the bombardment all day through field glasses. That night Key couldn't sleep but paced the deck watching "the bombs bursting in air."

Shortly before dawn on the fourteenth, the shelling stopped. Key couldn't tell what was happening, though, because a heavy fog blanketed the fort. Finally, around 7:00 A.M., the fog lifted enough for him to see that "our flag was still there." Torn and battered, the huge banner floated above Fort McHenry in the morning breeze.

Key and Dr. Beanes rejoiced that the fort had not surrendered. Later that morning they learned

56

that the British attack on Baltimore had failed, and the British fleet was withdrawing. They were free to go ashore.

Key was filled with patriotic enthusiasm. Some say that he began writing "The Star-Spangled Banner" while sailing back to Baltimore. He finished the first draft in his hotel room that night.

Key read the poem to his sister, who lived in Baltimore, and she insisted that he send it to a local newspaper. It was published on September 21, 1814, with the note that it should be sung to the tune of a British drinking song, "To Anacreon in Heaven." But the note didn't say who had written the poem; Francis Scott Key had been too modest to sign it.

The song spread quickly around the country. First the navy and then the army adopted it as their anthem. But more than a hundred years passed before President Woodrow Wilson named it our official national anthem in 1916.

Today the battle-scarred flag that inspired Francis Scott Key to write "The Star-Spangled Banner" can be seen at the National Museum of American History in Washington, D.C.

When Alaska was admitted to the Union as the forty-ninth state on July 4, 1959, army and navy units reenacted the bombardment of Fort McHenry that Key saw. However, "the rockets' red glare" on that occasion was caused by fireworks, not shells.

Here is the opening stanza of "The Star-Spangled Banner," the best-known of all American patriotic songs.

Oh, say, can you see by the dawn's early light,
What so proudly we hailed at the twilight's
   last gleaming?
Whose broad stripes and bright stars, through the
   perilous fight,
O'er the ramparts we watched were so
   gallantly streaming?
And the rockets' red glare, the bombs bursting in air,
Gave proof through the night that our flag was
   still there.
Oh, say, does that star-spangled banner yet wave
O'er the land of the free and the home of the brave?

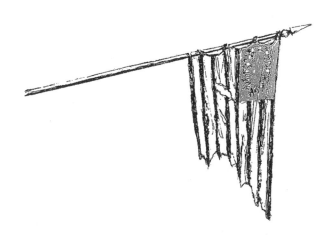

Uncle Sam

Marching at the head of many Fourth of July parades is a man or boy dressed in a familiar costume. He wears a tailcoat, striped trousers, and a beard. On his head sits a tall top hat decorated with the stars and stripes. Everyone knows at once that he is Uncle Sam, the symbol of the United States.

But not everyone knows that there was a real Uncle Sam. His name was Samuel Wilson and he was born in Arlington, Massachusetts, in 1766. Sam Wilson's father and two older brothers all fought in the Revolutionary War. Sam himself ran away from home at the age of fourteen to enlist in the army.

After the war, Sam moved to Troy, New York, where he started a meatpacking business. He worked hard and soon became known in the community for his honesty and common sense. When

U.S. Wilson

the War of 1812 broke out, Sam began to supply meat to the U.S. Army.

One day a group of officials, including the governor of New York, visited Sam Wilson's plant. They noticed that all the barrels of beef were stamped with the initials "U.S." and asked what they stood for.

"Uncle Sam," a workman said.

"Uncle Sam who?" a reporter in the group asked.

"Why, Uncle Sam Wilson, of course — the man who's supplying the army with its meat."

The reporter included this story in an account of the visit that he wrote for a New York City newspaper. It was reprinted elsewhere, and soon people were calling everything from beef to cannonballs "Uncle Sam's." Later, soldiers began saying they were in "Uncle Sam's Army."

After the War of 1812, Uncle Sam gradually became a national symbol. He first appeared in political cartoons in the 1830s. At that time he was portrayed as a young man, without gray hair or a beard. He didn't wear a top hat or tailcoat, either. The stars and stripes were on his shirt.

60

Some say that Dan Rice, a clown of the 1840s, thought up the Uncle Sam costume we know. Rice also walked on stilts to make Uncle Sam look taller and more commanding. The well-known cartoonist Thomas Nast drew the first picture of Uncle Sam with chin whiskers in 1869. From that time on he has always had a beard.

One of the most famous portraits of Uncle Sam was the army recruiting poster painted by James Montgomery Flagg during World War I. Uncle Sam is looking straight out at the viewer, pointing a finger, and saying "I Want You!" The model for this Uncle Sam was the artist himself.

In recent years some people have criticized the use of Uncle Sam as a symbol of the United States. He may represent the stern farmers who built Colonial America, they say. But he doesn't convey the breadth and depth of today's America. To many at home and abroad, he may seem more like a bully than a friend.

Despite such criticisms, Uncle Sam lives on as a symbol. The memory of the real Uncle Sam is being kept alive, too. Samuel Wilson's birthday, September 13, has been proclaimed "Uncle Sam's Day" in New York State. And in 1961, the U.S. Congress adopted a special resolution. It saluted "Uncle Sam" Wilson of Troy, New York, as the father of our national symbol — one of the most important symbols of Independence Day.

The Eagle

On banners and floats in Fourth of July parades, there often appears the image of our national bird, the bald eagle.

Actually, the bald eagle isn't bald. It has white feathers on top of its head. But when English settlers first came to America and saw the bird, the word *bald* meant "white," not "hairless."

The bald eagle is one of the largest birds in the world. Adults stand three feet high. The male weighs eight pounds and has a wingspread of about seven feet. The female is larger; she may weigh as much as twelve pounds and have a wingspread of twelve feet.

Because of their size and strength, eagles have been a symbol of power since ancient times. An eagle was the emblem of one of the Pharaohs of Egypt. Gold eagles perched atop the standards that Roman armies carried into battle.

However, there were long debates in the U.S. Congress before the eagle was adopted as our national bird in 1782. Many felt that the eagle, which had been the emblem of kings and empires, wasn't a good symbol for a new, young democracy.

One of the eagle's strongest opponents was Benjamin Franklin, who said, "The eagle is a bird of bad moral character. He does not get his living honestly. . . . too lazy to fish for himself, he watches the labor of the fishing hawk, and when that diligent bird has at last taken a fish, the bald eagle pursues him and takes it from him."

Franklin was exaggerating the eagle's bad habits in order to make his point. Eagles do sometimes seize food from smaller birds, but they catch their own food, too.

Franklin went on to suggest that the turkey would be a better choice as our national bird. "The turkey is in comparison a much more respectable bird, a true original native of America. Eagles have been found in all countries, but the turkey is peculiar to ours. . . ."

At last Congress reached a compromise. It selected the bald eagle, a bird that was found only on the North American continent and was unknown in Europe.

In 1782 bald eagles were plentiful and had no enemies except for an occasional human hunter. That situation didn't last long. As the United

States expanded westward, the birds were hunted ruthlessly for sport, and because they were predators. Eventually they became quite rare.

In 1940 Congress passed a law forbidding the capture or killing of a bald eagle. However, people kept on shooting the birds when they thought they could get away with it.

At the same time, widespread use of pesticides like DDT drastically lowered the eagles' birth rate. When female eagles ate fish poisoned by DDT, they produced eggs with shells too thin for hatching. By 1970, wildlife biologists estimated that there were fewer than a thousand bald eagles left in the United States.

Since the use of DDT was banned in 1972, the eagle population has begun to increase. Today, biologists think that at least 4,000 to 5,000 bald eagles live in the United States. These magnificent birds are not yet out of danger, but their future looks brighter than it did a few decades ago.

Meanwhile, millions of bald eagles appear with wings outstretched on coins, postage stamps, and dollar bills, and on the Great Seal of the United States. Thousands more are featured in Fourth of July newspaper and magazine stories, and in holiday celebrations of all kinds.

The Liberty Bell

★ ★ ☆

To many people, nothing symbolizes American independence as much as the Liberty Bell. Fourth of July fireworks often trace the outline of the Liberty Bell against the night sky. And almost every Independence Day parade includes a replica of the Bell on one of the floats.

The Liberty Bell wasn't known by that name when it arrived from England in September 1752. It was called the State House Bell, since it had been ordered for the new State House in Philadelphia.

Before the bell was raised to the top of the State House tower, it was hung from a temporary stand in the yard. People wanted to hear it ring, so one morning the bell was tested. While a crowd looked on, a smiling bellringer stepped up to the bell and swung its heavy clapper. A loud *bong* resounded through the air, but almost at once the

65

bellringer's smile changed to a worried frown. For a crack had split the rim and raced up the side of the bell.

Everyone was horrified. Some wanted to send the ruined bell back to England and order a replacement. Others thought that would take too long. At last it was decided to recast the bell in Philadelphia. John Stow, who owned a brass foundry that made everything from candlesticks to kettles, was hired to do the job. He took on John Pass as his assistant.

Pass and Stow broke the original bell into small pieces with sledgehammers so they could melt down the metal. Then they made new molds, poured in the metal, and recast the bell in Stow's foundry.

However, this first recasting wasn't a success. When the new bell was hung in the State House tower in April 1753, it made only a dull *bonk* when struck. Someone said it sounded like two coal scuttles being banged together.

So Pass and Stow took down the bell and started all over again. They worked quickly, and the third bell was ready by June. It was hung in the State House tower, and everyone in the yard below waited breathlessly as it was struck. They smiled when the bell gave out a loud, echoing *bong-g-g.*

On the side of the bell there is an inscription

from the Bible: "Proclaim Liberty throughout the land to all the Inhabitants Thereof" (Leviticus 25:10). Many people think this refers to the Declaration of Independence. But of course it couldn't, since it was carved on the bell twenty-three years before the Declaration was written. It refers instead to the freedom of religion that all citizens of Pennsylvania enjoyed.

Also on the bell is a statement that it was ordered for the State House of Pennsylvania, the names of Pass and Stow, and the year the bell was made. Someone made a mistake, though, and misspelled the word *Pennsylvania*. To this day it appears as "Pensylvania" on the side of the Liberty Bell.

From 1753 until 1776, the bell summoned public officials to meetings at the State House. It was rung often during sessions of the Second Continental Congress. But there is no record that it was rung on July 4, 1776, the day the Declaration of Independence was adopted.

Many people mistakenly believe that the Liberty Bell did ring loud and long on that day because of a story that was published in 1846. According to the story, an old, white-haired bellringer waited all afternoon in the steeple of the State House for word that the Declaration had been adopted. As he waited, he kept muttering to himself, "They'll never do it, they'll never do it!"

Suddenly a boy came racing up the tower steps. "They've signed!" he shouted. "Ring, Grandfather! Ring for Liberty!"

The old man's face broke into a huge smile. He grasped the bell ropes and gave them a mighty tug. The sound of the State House Bell rang out, carrying the glad news to everyone in Philadelphia.

It makes a good story, but there is no evidence that it really happened on July 4, 1776. We do know, however, that the State House Bell rang on July 8 to announce the first public reading of the Declaration. And that night it rang in celebration with all the other bells of Philadelphia.

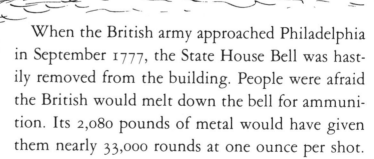

When the British army approached Philadelphia in September 1777, the State House Bell was hastily removed from the building. People were afraid the British would melt down the bell for ammunition. Its 2,080 pounds of metal would have given them nearly 33,000 rounds at one ounce per shot.

The State House Bell and ten other large city bells were loaded onto sturdy farmers' wagons and covered with straw. Then they were smuggled out of Philadelphia in the middle of the night so that British spies wouldn't know what was going on.

The wagons carrying the bells joined a convoy of 700 wagons loaded with refugees and goods. All of them headed northwest, away from the British army. Just as the convoy reached Bethlehem, Pennsylvania, on September 24, the wagon with the State House Bell broke down under its great weight.

The bell was transferred to another wagon and taken on to Allentown. There it was hidden in the basement of the Zion High German Reformed Church. The church itself was used as a military hospital for wounded soldiers from George Washington's army.

The State House Bell stayed in Allentown until the British left Philadelphia in June 1778. Then it was shipped back to Philadelphia along with the other city bells, and was rehung in the State House steeple. It rang when General Cornwallis of Great Britain surrendered to George Washington at Yorktown in 1781. It rang when the United States signed a peace treaty with Britain in 1783. And it rang over and over again when the U.S. Constitution was adopted in 1788.

The State House Bell kept on ringing on important occasions until July 8, 1835. On that morning it was tolling for the funeral procession of John Marshall, chief justice of the U.S. Supreme Court, when suddenly it cracked for the second time. Strangely enough, it was fifty-nine years to the day since the bell had rung out to celebrate the first reading of the Declaration of Independence.

The bell remained silent until 1846. Then the edges of the crack were filed down so that they wouldn't vibrate against each other, and the bell was rung on George Washington's birthday. At first it gave out loud, clear notes, but then the crack spread. After that, the bell could never be rung again.

But even though it was now silent for good, the bell lived on as a national symbol. It was first

called "the Liberty Bell" in an antislavery booklet published in 1839. The new name quickly took hold. In 1852, on the 100th anniversary of its arrival in Philadelphia, the Liberty Bell was put on display in the State House, which was now known as Independence Hall. The bell was placed on a pedestal with thirteen sides to represent the thirteen original states.

Why did the Liberty Bell become such a strong symbol of American freedom and independence? Perhaps because, unlike the Declaration of Independence, it was a three-dimensional object that could be seen and touched. Thousands of Americans and people from other countries came to view the bell when it was displayed at the great Centennial Exhibition in Philadelphia in 1876.

After that exhibition closed, the Liberty Bell traveled to many other cities. It was shown in New Orleans in 1885, in Chicago in 1893, in Boston in 1903, and in St. Louis in 1904.

Millions of people saw the bell on its tours around the country. It rode on a flat, open railroad car surrounded by a protective railing. The bell

was suspended from a wooden yoke with the words "1776 — Proclaim Liberty" lettered on it. Flowers, ribbons, and evergreen wreaths decorated the yoke and the flatcar.

As the Liberty Bell traveled on, people back in Philadelphia became more and more concerned about its safety. They feared that the bumping and jolting of the railroad would lengthen the crack in its side.

In 1915 the bell made one final trip to an exposition in San Francisco after 200,000 schoolchildren signed a petition asking that it be sent. Upon its return to Philadelphia, the bell was examined carefully. When it was discovered that the crack had widened, word went out: the Liberty Bell will travel no more. It has stayed in Philadelphia ever since.

Meanwhile, other bells rang in the Liberty Bell's place. As part of the Centennial celebrations of 1876, a wealthy merchant, Henry Seybert, gave money for a new bell to be installed in the tower of Independence Hall. The bell weighed 13,000 pounds — a thousand for each of the thirteen colonies — and was made from four Civil War cannons, melted down. It chimed for the first time at 12:01 A.M. on July 4, 1876.

To honor the 200th anniversary of the Declaration of Independence, Queen Elizabeth II of

Queen Elizabeth II

England presented a Bicentennial Bell to the people of the United States in July 1976. It was made in the Whitechapel Foundry in London, the same foundry that cast the original Liberty Bell. On its side are inscribed the words "Let Freedom Ring!"

At the presentation, Queen Elizabeth said: "It seems to me that Independence Day, the Fourth of July, should be celebrated as much in Britain as in America. Not in rejoicing at the separation of the American colonies from the British crown, but in sincere gratitude to the Founding Fathers of this great Republic for having taught Britain a very valuable lesson. . . . We learned to respect the right of others to govern themselves in their own ways."

The Bicentennial Bell now hangs in a simple brick belfry that is part of the Independence Park Visitors Center in Philadelphia. It is rung every day at 11:00 A.M. and 3:00 P.M., and on special occasions.

But it is the silent Liberty Bell to which hundreds of thousands of visitors still flock every year. Since New Year's Eve 1976, it has been displayed in a modern pavilion on the grassy mall below Independence Hall. Guides in the pavilion encourage people to touch the smooth surface of the bell and feel a part of it.

In 1962, author Eric Sloane started a campaign to have the nation celebrate the Fourth of July by

73

ringing bells all across the country at 2:00 P.M. The Liberty Bell soon became the focal point of this campaign, which gained many supporters.

Now, on the Fourth of July, descendants of the men who signed the Declaration of Independence gather at the Liberty Bell pavilion. Often they are children. Promptly at two o'clock they tap the Liberty Bell gently with rubber-tipped hammers. At the same time the Centennial Bell atop Independence hall chimes thirteen times, once for each of the thirteen colonies.

Special Fourth of July Celebrations

Over the years, special ways of celebrating Independence Day have sprung up in many different parts of the United States.

In Bristol, Rhode Island, there is a Fireman's Muster. Fire engine companies from all over New England gather to take part in a water-squirting competition. As hundreds watch, each company aims its hoses to see who can shoot streams of water the highest and farthest.

Several states and localities honor native Americans on July 4. Wisconsin has designated the Fourth as Indian Rights Day, and recommends that appropriate ceremonies be held throughout the state. In Flagstaff, Arizona, native Americans from more than twenty tribes stage a huge, three-day All Indian Powwow over the July 4 weekend. Thousands of Indians participate in tribal dances and an action-filled rodeo while crowds of tourists and local people watch.

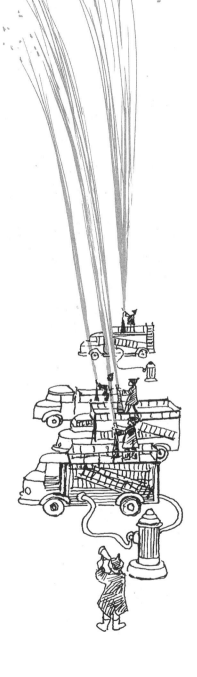

75

The annual Eskimo games are held every July 4 in Kotzebue, Alaska, north of the Arctic Circle. Expert sailors compete for prizes in the kayak races. There is a special prize for the Eskimo who catches the biggest beluga whale.

Many other sporting events are scheduled for July 4. Racing car fans come from all over the country to see Colorado's annual auto race up the slopes of 14,000-foot Pike's Peak. Other fans travel to Florida to watch the 400-mile stock car races at the Daytona International Speedway.

Two of the most unusual celebrations of Independence Day take place in Hannibal, Missouri, and Ontario, California. In Hannibal, Mark Twain's hometown, youngsters revive memories of Tom Sawyer by entering the National Fence Painting Contest. In Ontario, families bring their lunches to what is described as "the longest picnic table in the world." It runs for two miles along Ontario's Euclid Avenue. Sitting behind it, everyone has a front-row seat for the town's annual Fourth of July parade.

A unique Fourth of July ceremony has been staged every year since 1818 in the little eastern Pennsylvania town of Lititz. It is called the "Festival of Candles."

During the winter, the people of Lititz make thousands of candles in old-fashioned tin molds. On the evening of July 4, they take the candles to

76

Lititz Springs Park and arrange them in the shapes of stars, wheels, crescents, and pyramids.

Visitors from miles around look on as a Queen of the Candles is chosen from the senior class of the town high school. Then the candles are lit, transforming the entire park into a fairyland. Some are set afloat in small boats on the park lake. All the flickering lights make a lovely climax to the Fourth of July.

Anniversaries are always special. So it isn't surprising that spectacular Independence Day celebrations were held on the 100th anniversary of the Declaration of Independence in 1876, and on the 200th anniversary in 1976.

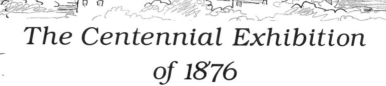

The Centennial Exhibition of 1876

★ ☆ ☆

Philadelphia's Centennial celebration in 1876 lasted for six months. That was how long the Centennial International Exhibition, the first such exhibition in the United States, was open to the public. All the states and thirty-nine foreign countries had displays at the Exhibition, which covered 236 acres in Philadelphia's Fairmount Park.

President Ulysses S. Grant opened the Exhibition on May 10, 1876, by pulling a lever that started a 1,500-horsepower Corliss steam engine. This huge engine provided power for all the displays in Machinery Hall, the main building at the fair. It quickly became one of the most popular items in the entire exhibition. Another machine that always drew a crowd was Alexander Graham Bell's new invention, the telephone.

Other buildings at the Exhibition focused on agriculture, education, architecture, and the achieve-

78

ments of American women. European countries lent famous art works. There were also arts and crafts on display from Latin America, Africa, and the Far East. One of the most popular paintings at the Exhibition, as mentioned before, was Archibald Willard's *The Spirit of '76*.

France had intended to give the Statue of Liberty to the United States as a Centennial present. Construction was delayed because all the money for the statue hadn't been raised. However, Liberty's right arm holding the torch was completed in time for the Centennial Exhibition. Visitors excitedly climbed up a flight of stairs inside the giant arm and had their pictures taken on the balcony surrounding the torch.

By the time the Centennial Exhibition closed on November 10, 1876, it had been seen by almost ten million people. That was one-fifth of the total population of the United States at the time.

President Johnson

President Nixon

The Bicentennial of 1976

☆ ☆ ☆

Plans for the Bicentennial celebrations of 1976 were begun ten years earlier, on July 4, 1966, when President Lyndon B. Johnson established the American Revolution Bicentennial Commission.

In 1970 the Commission delivered its report to President Richard M. Nixon. The report urged "all groups within our society to re-examine our origins, our values, and the meaning of America — to take pride in our accomplishments and to dramatize our development." It also encouraged everyone to seek ways "to help make America 'the more perfect union' and to improve the quality of life for our third century."

In the next few years more than twenty-five million Americans helped to get the country ready for the Bicentennial. Historic areas and downtown districts in many cities were restored. New civic centers and museums were built, and old ones were expanded. Historical festivals and exhibits were presented.

Finally the great day arrived: July 4, 1976, the 200th anniversary of the adoption of the Declaration of Independence.

The nation's celebrations officially began atop Mars Hill in northeastern Maine. There the rising sun first struck U.S. soil at 4:31 A.M. While more than five hundred tourists and local farmers cheered, National Guardsmen fired a fifty-gun salute and raised the American flag.

In Philadelphia, 25,000 people crowded into the square behind Independence Hall where the Declaration of Independence was first read publicly in 1776. They heard President Gerald R. Ford deliver the keynote address. "Liberty is a living flame to be fed," the President said, "not dead ashes to be revered, even in a Bicentennial year."

Throughout the country there were serious celebrations of the holiday. In Seattle, five boys reenacted the raising of the U.S. flag on Iwo Jima's Mount Suribachi during World War II. Civil War experts in Pennsylvania re-created the Battle of Gettysburg, which took place from July 1 to July 4, 1863. Mass naturalization ceremonies were held for 7,141 new American citizens in Miami, 2,300 in Chicago, and over 1,000 in Detroit.

There were silly, just-for-fun events, too, and many records were broken. The largest cherry

President Ford

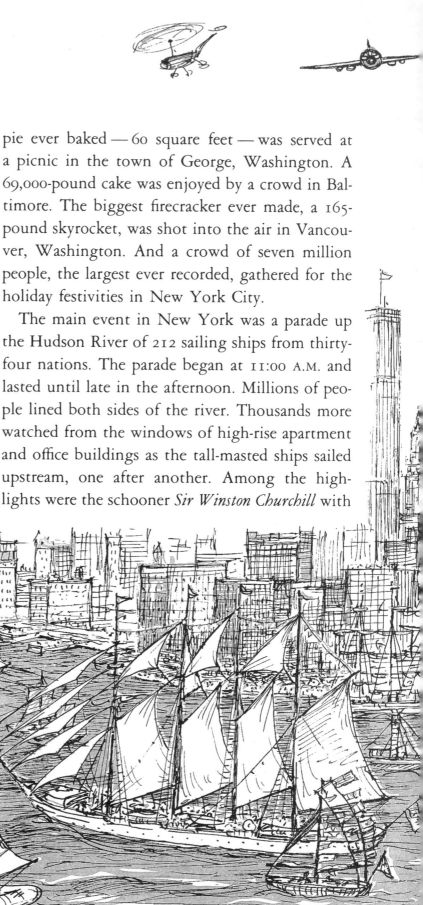

pie ever baked — 60 square feet — was served at a picnic in the town of George, Washington. A 69,000-pound cake was enjoyed by a crowd in Baltimore. The biggest firecracker ever made, a 165-pound skyrocket, was shot into the air in Vancouver, Washington. And a crowd of seven million people, the largest ever recorded, gathered for the holiday festivities in New York City.

The main event in New York was a parade up the Hudson River of 212 sailing ships from thirty-four nations. The parade began at 11:00 A.M. and lasted until late in the afternoon. Millions of people lined both sides of the river. Thousands more watched from the windows of high-rise apartment and office buildings as the tall-masted ships sailed upstream, one after another. Among the highlights were the schooner *Sir Winston Churchill* with

its all-female crew, an exact replica of a Viking ship with a striped sail, and a full-scale model of Christopher Columbus' flagship, the *Santa Maria*.

President Ford, who had flown from Philadelphia by helicopter, reviewed the parade from the deck of the aircraft carrier *U.S.S. Forrestal*. At 2:00 P.M. he rang the ship's bells thirteen times to honor the thirteen original colonies.

At the same moment the Liberty Bell in Philadelphia was tapped gently with a rubber mallet. The Centennial Bell in the steeple of Independence Hall rang out loud and clear. And hundreds of other bells all across the country pealed in a joyful national chorus.

1776–1976, HAPPY BIRTHDAY, U.S.A.

The climax to the Bicentennial celebrations came on the evening of July 4.

More than 400,000 people crowded onto the Esplanade along the Charles River in Boston to hear the Boston Pops give an outdoor concert. The highlight of the concert was Tchaikovsky's *1812 Overture,* during which howitzers boomed, church bells rang, and fireworks lit up the scene.

In New York City, fireworks were fired from barges in the harbor and fell in showers of light around the Statue of Liberty. At the end of the spectacle a helicopter flew over the statue, towing behind it a flag made of red, white, and blue lights. Loudspeakers played "The Star-Spangled Banner," and the crowds along the shore burst into song.

Three thousand miles away in San Francisco, fireworks shot up into the sky above Candlestick Park and Alcatraz Island.

The biggest fireworks display of all was staged in Washington, D.C. More than thirty-three tons of fireworks rose into the sky above the Mall, near the Washington Monument, and exploded in light patterns of all sizes, shapes, and colors. At the close, a battery of laser guns spelled out on the clouds, "1776–1976, Happy Birthday, U.S.A."

Not every Fourth of July can be as exciting as the Bicentennial. But next Independence Day, and all the ones after it, will be celebrated with the same symbols — the flag, the bald eagle, Uncle Sam, the Liberty Bell. There will be parades, picnics, and band concerts. And fireworks will flash again across the night sky.

Each new July 4 gives us a chance to show our love for our country. It also offers us an opportunity to examine ourselves as Americans. We can look back at the road we have traveled, and decide what direction we want to take in the future.

The first July 4 came about only after much conflict and argument. The main question then was "Should we break with Britain or try to work out our differences?" Today there are still arguments on the Fourth. But now the question most people ask is "Have we as a nation achieved the goals that were set forth in the Declaration of Independence?"

It may take another two hundred years before we agree on the answer to that question. Meanwhile, we will be reminded of it every time we join in celebrating the Fourth of July.

Important Events That Have Taken Place on July 4

July 4, 1776	The Declaration of Independence was adopted.
July 4, 1802	The United States Military Academy at West Point was opened.
July 4, 1817	Governor DeWitt Clinton of New York dug the first shovelful of earth for the Erie Canal.
July 4, 1828	Charles Carroll, the last surviving signer of the Declaration of Independence, turned over the first shovelful of dirt for the construction of the Baltimore and Ohio Railroad.
July 4, 1850	The cornerstone of the Washington Monument in Washington, D.C., was laid.

July 4, 1876	The United States celebrated the 100th anniversary of the adoption of the Declaration of Independence.
July 4, 1883	"Buffalo Bill" Cody's first Wild West Show opened at North Platte, Nebraska.
July 4, 1884	The government of France presented the Statue of Liberty to the United States.
July 4, 1903	President Theodore Roosevelt opened the first trans-Pacific cable with a message that traveled around the world in twelve minutes.
July 4, 1946	The Philippine Islands, which had been a territory of the United States, became a free and independent republic.
July 4, 1959	The 49-star flag signaling Alaska's entry into the United States was first flown over Fort McHenry in Baltimore, Maryland.
July 4, 1960	The 50-star flag signaling Hawaii's entry into the United States was first flown over Fort McHenry.

July 4, 1976   The United States celebrated the 200th anniversary of the adoption of the Declaration of Independence.

July 4, 1982   The space shuttle *Columbia* made a successful landing after seven days in orbit around the Earth.

Index